D0398251

THE SMELL OF LIFE

That's the poet's business—not to talk
in vague categories, but to write particularly,
as a physician works upon a patient,
upon the thing before him, in the particular
to discover the universal.
—William Carlos Williams

The Story Of My Life

I knew they'd be closed
—it was ten past five.

I went there anyhow.

Sure-enough, the door was locked.
But they let me in.

THE SMELL OF LIFE

Morty Sklar

poems

1969 TO 2005

The Spirit That Moves Us Press
ESTABLISHED 1975

Jackson Heights, Queens,
New York City : 2008

Acknowledgements

JAMES C. HARRISON, DUSTJACKET ART
VICTOR BIONDO, DR. EFRÉN RAMÍREZ, JACK MCNEELY,
AND FREDDIE, SAVING MY LIFE

"Jarashow's" appeared in *Brother Songs* (Holy Cow! Press)
"Ode To The Sun," in *A–Z: Contemporary American Poets* (Swallow Press)
"Red And Blue Noon," *The Night We Stood Up For Our Rights*
 (Toothpaste Press, now called Coffee House Press)
"The E Train," *Little Caesar* magazine
"My Pants," *Mid-Atlantic Review*
"Culture," *Off The Cuffs* (Soft Skull Press)
"Charlie 'Bird' Parker," *The First Poem* (Snapper Press)
"Sometimes A Sandwich Is Not Just A Sandwich," *The Actualist Anthology*
 (The Spirit That Moves Us Press)
"You Showed Me Yours / I Showed You Mine," *Riverside* (Emmess Press)
"I Put The Telephone Back On Its Receiver," *Abraxas* magazine
"Ode To Goofy," *The New Pioneer Cooperative* magazine
"Making Beans To Bruckner's Ninth," *Open Places* magazine
"Caffeine, Nicotine, Meat, and Warm Bodies Partaking Of Nourishment,"
 The Empty Window Review
"Things I Thought Were Bad For Us," *Legionnaire* magazine
"On Being A Grown-up," *Lips* magazine
"The Story Of My Life," *World Letter* magazine
"My Mother Said She Was Held Back," *Alzheimer's Association Newsletter*

Library of Congress Cataloging-in-Publication Data

Sklar, Morty, 1935-
 The smell of life : poems, 1969 to 2005 / Morty Sklar. – 1st ed.
  p. cm. – (Outstanding author series ; no. 7)
 "Also offered as volume 14 of The spirit that moves us"–T.p. verso.
 Summary: "Inspired by the natural-voice aesthetics of the Iowa City Actualists
(of which he was a seminal writer and editor), the Beats, and the New York
Poets, Morty Sklar writes with humor, intimacy and original insight in this
thirty-six-year collection of poems addressing everything from heroin addiction
to honor, innocent joy to mortal resignation, loneliness to everlasting love"
–Provided by publisher.
 ISBN 978-0-930370-56-5 (alk. paper)
 I. Spirit that moves us. II. Title.
 PS3569.K56S64 2008
 811'.854–dc22   2008013005

for Gratitude

Contents

chronological order

I. After My Fall From Gracelessness

II. The Road Taken

III. Following My Nose

IV. My 1980s

V. You *Can* Go Home Again

green
press
INITIATIVE

The Spirit That Moves Us Press is committed to preserving
ancient forests and natural resources. We elected to print this
title on 30% post consumer recycled paper, processed chlorine
free. As a result, for this printing, we have saved:

1 Trees (40' tall and 6-8" diameter)
479 Gallons of Wastewater
193 Kilowatt Hours of Electricity
53 Pounds of Solid Waste
104 Pounds of Greenhouse Gases

The Spirit That Moves Us Press made this paper choice because
our printer, Thomson-Shore, Inc., is a member of Green Press
Initiative, a nonprofit program dedicated to supporting authors,
publishers, and suppliers in their efforts to reduce their use of
fiber obtained from endangered forests.

For more information, visit www.greenpressinitiative.org

I
After My Fall From Gracelessness

Red and Blue Noon

with Harlem in mind

The red and blue, properties of neon and argon,
elements amiable to bars and taverns and other places of night,
and common to Pluto, Neptune, and the moons of Jupiter,
which do not so much shine, as glow, in the city.

Unlike the elevated train, these signs fit gently
into the midnight of our sky,
the gases charged through tubes of clear glass
that bend and twist like an artist's hand,
and are seen, too, from many darkened streets away
by old people at their windows.

And from every direction, journeys
of a few hundred feet, or thousands,
to enter beneath them
to warm exhalations of smoke,
the smell of fermented grain,
to music, strangers, and friends.

1969

Closer

for Ingrid, first love

"Now"
    goes a song, "everything's easy
    —you're in love."
Yeah?—it's a problem whether to cut my hair.
    And last night I walked hungrily
past Asia de Cuba   Gourmet Treats   White Tower
—imagine *me* undecided about what to eat.

I've been down before,
the high spots in my life having been

    Pushing Gunther, the super's son,
    Going to Chinatown with Mom and Dad
        for shrimp with lobster sauce and penny arcades,
    Making kids in class laugh,
    Catching fly balls at Greg's Field,
    Stealing classroom cookie money at night,
    Breaking into the Hobby Hub for airplanes and money,
    Going to the store for Grandma
        and being served by that silent Polish lady
        golden soup with yellow chicken feet,
    Listening to the big bands on "Milkman's Matinée,"
    Squatting on Gilson's chest
        —he who beat-up my kid brother
        —everyone shouting, "whip his ass,"
        but my wanting no more
        what I'd wanted before...

    Meeting God without a rabbi, under my bunk
        in the Fort Bragg North Carolina army stockade,

Willing, if not ready and able in '60 to conquer,
    working the lunch counters of N.Y.C. Whelans,
Shooting-up methedrine, and beholding Joyce's fair skin
    red in the glow of a bath towel,
Talking-up a storm with highly esteemed friends…

Walking in unlonely solitude on 3rd Avenue snow
    embracing as a lover the slavery
        that stopped   the machinery   of everything.

Resting at last
    after days of first Tombs junk kick
    and the illogical glory of
        CLEAN again
  then
        Phoenix House
           and back to work and beginnings.

I met you, Lovely,
along the way
and found, when you left,
that love wasn't magic
—no more than everything.

October 1970

Jarashow's

ancient store on Jamaica Avenue

Hand truck up-
    on which I throw cartons of tools and hardware
    destined for that place, high-ceilinged of pressed tin,
    with steel drawers of dozens and grosses of nuts,
    bolts, screws, pipes, fittings, nails…

At 160th Street and 91st Avenue,
    a block from the old Jamaica elevated train,
    I unload our '70 Chevy station wagon
    quickly, like my father, but not because the cartons
    —pieces of my life—are my future.

Old woman in black shawl, zinc gray hair
    and gray face, tells me:
        "I remember you, you were six
        when you came around with your father."

Driving back through Union Turnpike towns
    past Utopia Parkway homes, I speak to Dad
    in my head: Mrs. Jarashow said she remembers me.
    —I told her, you mean my brother; she said
    "No, you were six when you came with your father."
        He'll be pleased, for what came between us
        is gone, there's time to talk with my father
        who at thirteen headed a fatherless brood,
            rushing
                till now.
    I having been well-fed
        went another way, blessed it comes to this
        as in old times when sons came home.

When Jarashow's was new
    with maple counters and zinc storage bins,
    my father was selling hardware and tools from job lots
    stored in my grandparents' basement.
        At thirty-five he'd failed, was starting-out again
        hustling in the streets of Jersey City,
        lower Manhattan, Elmhurst…
        —my father who (he never told me until I too
        did it) took chances, made a bundle in woolens
        on daring, lost, bought a barrel of peanuts
        and peddled them from a furnished room.

Father, see,
    I too have aimed for what I want
    —a little late and unsure, but now
    that doesn't matter.
        We have time before kaddish;
        everything's okay
        between you and me.

November 1970

Bed

In my $40/month room, West 20th Street

I'm sitting next to it now
foot upon it
—can't help that, it's everywhere
in this room here.

Lean upon it, read upon it
make love listen to the radio
upon it; not least of all's
sleeping on it.

I get up in the morning
to get a lot done, and now
I'm 35

November 1970

Giovanni Gabucci

a.k.a. John Cabbage

Poet John Cabbage talking
    about Max Bodenheim,
    harvesting the Dakotas,
    shipping out to sea,

    about organizing unions
    before there were any,
    about Bob White and his fight
    for the underdog.

John Cabbage getting beat-up,
    dumped on a foreign shore,
    walking the Bowery, talking
    with Charlie Chaplin,
    writing poems on garbage scows,
    interviewed by Dag Hammarskjöld.

John Cabbage talking about
    contemporary poetry,
    "goddamn hippies,"
    thinking the underdog
    has lost.

February 1971

The E Train

I am the engineer

I speed along rails
through 30-watt undergrounds,
beneath the river in constant night,
over sewers, blackened timbers,
Bethlehem beams…

I arrive and depart, arrive and depart.
Faces on platforms emerge from the tunnel…
　　Though I know
it's not my dark cab they see,
but the powder-blue E,
I have waited for them,
they have waited for me.

March 1971

II
The Road Taken

On The Way To Iowa City

Warming my hands by
the heat of the engine,
riding the highways of Butler Pee Ay
    doing 55 on 68
    all the way to 80,
    riding the hills of Penn State a.m.

What more could I ask in a 5 a.m. night,
what more could I want in the fog of the morn
when my 'cycle stutters
    on an Alleg-
    he
    ny
    hill
and I kick the gear down,
she grabs, pulls

    to cows in a pasture
    to sun coming up

August 1971

My Pants

My pants are getting old
in the tradition of the Beats

—no rainbow colors, no patches,
and I reach for them getting out of bed
and put them on

February 1972

23

The Night We Stood Up For Our Rights

A bell rang   rang   rang   rang
as the Rock Island locomotive chugged   chugged
while we ran down to the A & P market
to demand peanut butter.

    We were shown a Cadillac
and Cadillac jam, and told that with two coupons
we could get extra jam
but we knew where they were coming from

    so we locked elbows
and through the force of our conviction
united them with us.
The blond manager with crew-cut and glasses
grinned, and then the others.

    Jim looked at me.
    What now? he said.

    "*Jelly*, man,
    GRAPE jelly"

February 1972

Charlie "Bird" Parker

Exploiting the medium
for all it's got

    Bird flying forever

wait a minute
I'll get my saxophone

    Lady Be Good
    in four-four,
    play a warped piano till it straightens out

I'm not always lonely
are you?

    bablee *doo* dah
    bablee *doo* dah

October 1972

To The White Lady
(Heroin)

A rag surrogate were you
I suckled at your chickenwire breasts.

My pet, I fed you
sweetmeat and lobster tails
while I ate Gainesburgers;
mother's milk while I drank
dusty preserve jars of crooked stairs.
You were cruel you were demanding
like a gum machine in the subway.

In your arms I'd lain,
as comfortable as a concrete bench
under the East River bridge.

Lady, now should we meet,
I won't nod.

June 1973

26

Song Of Red Route

Sailing through mist,
a yellow light blinks at me.
Little Running Backpack arrives
at the bus stop as I do.

My windshield wiper waves
wildly at the sky;
brown wrinkled leaves blow
through the opened door.

At the corner a cape
flaps.
Rain drives some people crazy
—they run in front of my moving bus.

Students stand like flowers
trees dive into the earth
the mist rises
my bus moves on.

The brakes are working
The heat is working
EVERYTHING is working!

November 1973

Sometimes A Sandwich Is Not Just A Sandwich

rained-out at Delaware Water Gap
on my Honda 305 "Dream,"
New York City to Iowa City

What I enjoy most has been made rubbish of:
transistor radio, salami-and-cheese sandwich, sneakers.
Now when I think *sandwich*
I feel responsible.

With each postponement of going for a sandwich
I'm given a poem.

I'm sitting out here without a sandwich.
Moral decisions are made alone

      but together
      we're happy

August 1974

You Showed Me Yours / I Showed You Mine

You showed me toadstools and a thorn tree
    I showed you smokestacks and a highway
You made rhubarb pie and a long dress
    I made it out of the city
You listened to crickets, and corn grow
    I, to the radio
You'd lost your place in the sun
    I found one

You showed me patience and a smile
    I showed you I could stay awhile
You brought my eggs scrambled soft
    I brought you to the hayloft

You showed me your love so fine
I showed you mine.

1974

I Put The Telephone Back On Its Receiver

The coleus bloomed
    the lamp spoke to a book
a load of air poured through the transom
    the wandering jew climbed out of its pot
the blanket gathered and almost got out of bed
    an inverted mop spoke to something in the wall
posters and reminders hung by their fingertips
    out-of-breath

    and the refrigerator started-up
as the soft motor in my chest went thump
for the one billion four hundred forty-four million
eighty-six thousandth time

February 1975

III
Following My Nose

The Smell Of Life

Rubbing alcohol
and a breeze at an open window,
warm February day.

Rubbing alcohol
and infrared-heated beef mashed potatoes and string beans
much the same as rubbing alcohol
ham french fries and broccoli.

Later, on the way to the tv room or the gymnasium
in striped cotton robe
my breath tastes like dinner
like all the dinners.

The alcohol touches at once
tonsillectomy, Mother's hemorrhage,
my electroshock therapy, heroin, hepatitis,
and awakens fear
but is inexplicably reassuring
like the odor of gasoline and sewage
near lower west side service stations and piers
where our family car sometimes took us
to relatives across the river,
furry arm of my mother,
aftershave of my father,
standing midstream at the prow of the ferry
a breeze across our faces.

1976, ten years after my final trip
to Manhattan General detox

Ode To Goofy

Oh Goofy,
tap-dancing in the kitchen
in the moonlight of streetlight,
to the dripping faucet, a song
of environmental unconcern,
beauty of waste.

Oh Coney Island
25¢ laughing entrance to Fear
thrill of dying

a dozen clams on the half-shell
hot sauce

Daffy Duck saltwater taffy
3 shots for a quarter,
rag doll reward

Midnight of the eternal steeplechase,
trashed windy blacktop
of the sauerkraut mustard cotton candy night

Oh Light

Star travelers of Brooklyn
taking the subway home

continued

Moonlight on the oil slick,
Mark Twain of the green condom river,
Ellis Island ghosts
    Liberty

    Oh say
    can you see

February 1977

Making Beans To Bruckner's 9th

In the landscape of a gray Iowa day,
a ribbon of smoke rises into the winter sky.
That which bubbles thickly for hours in the belly of a pot,
later simmers in one's own belly, from which
the inspiration of beans and symphonies had arisen
and back into which the fruition of them goes.

Bruckner's 9th— "unfinished,"
as other ninth symphonies have been called
—but as a critic said: "Uncompleted, yes,
but *not* unfinished!"

    And what of beans?
—when should they be removed from the stove?
Not long after the addition of onions and garlic?
—or with an inspiration of fresh spinach?
Or are beans done only in theory
—the way parallel lines meet at infinity?

    And what of us?
Does the Great Chef take the uncompleted
and leave the unfinished behind?

March 1977

Mending

There's no thread in view, no darning needles
—there's only the mending woman
propped against the pillow on her bed
three hours before dawn.
No shirts, no socks, nothing but a landscape
of leaves and vines on the bed sheet beneath her.

What do I bring to her while her hands rest quietly
upon her nightgown, and the pale moon of the streetlight
bathes her north-facing window?
Oh sure, my socks are worn through, and there's
the shoulder of my knit shirt—snagged on a
splintered banister as I climbed her garret stairs...

She's looking toward the vertically-slatted closet
beneath the sloped ceiling
but I feel she is looking at me.
The silence gathers in my belly, shines
in the mending woman's face.

At dawn
I relish the feel of my big toe
through the hole in my sock.

April 1977

Give Me Hamburger Or Give Me Death

Hamburger and eggs, please.
What's a nice hamburger like you
    doing in a place like this?
Gee you have the loveliest hamburger.
We could make beautiful hamburger together.
Would you like to go to the hamburger tonight?
Is your hamburger living?
Did you go hamburger for the holidays?
My hamburger wouldn't start up this morning.
It's a lovely day for a hamburger.
Does your hamburger know you're here?
Does your hamburger bite?
Is your hamburger older than you?
Do you play the hamburger?
Why did the hamburger cross the road?
Excuse me, I have to make a hamburger.
A hamburger well done.
Is there a hamburger in the house?
Seek first the kingdom of hamburger.
Leave the key under the hamburger.
May I have change of a hamburger?
Make hamburger, not war.
A hamburger a day keeps the doctor away.
Hamburger makes the heart grow fonder.
Everything you wanted to know about hamburger
    but were afraid to ask.
I pledge allegiance to the hamburger.
Hamburger is a joy forever.

Spring 1977

Poem For My Immigrant Father In New York

At 7:30 a.m.
you went to work in your eightieth year.

Here, the traffic had barely begun;
the air that wafted through my window
was clear; I could hear
birds a block from my downtown room.

You went to work as you have
for sixty-seven years.
At the desktop typesetting machine in my place,
I was already at work
so I wouldn't be going home when done for the day.

You went to work this morning
you never came home.

September 1978

Ode To The Sun

You're sitting in Rossi's Cafe on Gilbert Street
—main drag, trucks, early a.m.
across from end-of-March puddled vacant lot

    sunlight hops skips and jumps off
rooftop shingle, to puddle, to semi windshield shatter
and dust diffused in window

    Home-fries, eggs sunny-side-up
ninety-three million miles from the sun

      The snow
has just melted here,
and light spreads like a cosmic *good* virus,
glinting off auburn coffee splashed on the floor,
tossed around in mop with sound waves
from transistor radio

You're a crystal receiver
hundreds of light years from nowhere

    near some puddles
next to the sun

March 1979, Iowa City

39

IV
My 1980s

Caffeine, Nicotine, Meat
and Warm Bodies Partaking Of Nourishment

This ain't the Sheepshead, with its quiche, espresso,
imported beer, classical music, art student paintings,
natural wood decor, outdoor tables, hanging plants,
exquisitely thin slivers of rich pie at mod prices
and stylishly slow service
    and this ain't Simmy's, with its arty patron photo
portraits, garbanzo bean burgers and hot apple cider
(10% juice, but swell glasses and a sprinkle of cinnamon)

—this is just old Hamburg Inn, in my adopted city
of Iowa City.

    I know I should have gone home as usual
after jogging and calisthenics, and made some stone-ground
whole wheat cornmeal buttermilk pancakes topped with
honey and peaches, and brewed some organic French roast
coffee, but shit, I'm a working man and a man living alone
—I just wanted someone to fix my meal, and,
hamburgers are in my genes, and an older woman in a dress
is in my memory bank. Besides, poison is good for you,
sometimes—hamburger and coffee give the liver and kidneys
a work-out just as the muscles and respiratory systems
are worked when labored with exercise.
And I like to ask someone once in a while, to pass the ketchup
or "Are you going to use that ashtray?" And it's nice
to leave the dishes for someone else to wash for a change;
even leaving a tip is a kind of communication.

    You wanna show-off your grandmother's dress?
or your Jordache jeans or raggedy neo-hippie cut-offs,
headband and slouch? —go to the Sheepshead or Simmy's

—someone there will appreciate you (or hate you
for being more different than they).
      But hey, you probably enjoy getting together
with your friends at a place you like. I'm no snob—
I'm not saying that Hamburg Inn is the end-all and be-all
of eating establishments. And, we might even run into
each other at a $1.50 flick at the Bijou—which at a
Greenwich Village "art" theatre would be $6.
Then someone might talk about *us,*
someone who eats at Mr. Steak.

July 1980

Rules

All day the sun shone, and all day I worked inside.
        Once I had a rule—live where the sun shines in.
My first exception by choice was a $4.80-per-week room
on Saint Mark's Place, Greenwich Village.
Other exceptions followed as life dictated.

        Here on North Johnson in Iowa City, there's some sun
—mostly in the bathroom, and in the living room briefly.
The rear south door is sunny when it's open:
not when it's cold outside or when I'm typesetting
and not with construction going on next door.

        Exceptions become as important as rules,
and my being expands a little more to make room for less,
as not long ago it made room for a wife,
and not long after, her departure,
and beginning long ago, for dreams, their frustration,
fulfillment, their discard, their disregard
of the dreamer.

        The soul can keep growing. It feeds on nothing
like a cactus, on anything like a homeless refugee,
on everything like a glutton.
It doesn't get skinny and it doesn't get fat
—it just gets, or is got.

The dreams that are gone…
the people who are gone…

        Today words
        shine in

                                        May 8, 1983

44

Time-Life, Un-incorporated

"Time—from the people who brought you
Life, Fortune, and *Money"* —a radio ad

Sun rays diffused through dusty window
stream over my shoulder
as I date my rent check January 1, 1982
—then cross-out the 2 and write 3.

I send my niece Jennifer a large-format book
of the solar system. She'll be eleven in a week.
In my wallet is a frayed photo of her curly-headed
intense two-year-old face staring up at my camera.

I stand on the rec center scale after a workout.
There's a table of "ideal" body weights
according to age. I look at the 35–49 range.
In a year I'll be in the last category.

    Monday—time for our boy scout troop meeting.
I'm to be tested for First Class Scout.
    Monday—time for a post-marital meeting
with my counselor.

I buy a pair of good leather shoes, navy surplus;
they wear-out.
    I get another pair. They wear out.
I leave my apartment on South Dubuque Street;
when I return, there's a post office there.
    I visit my friend Jim for the umpty-dumpth time
at his bookstore/apartment

continued

and stop by the post office afterwards
where there's a letter from him, from Singapore.

I'm excited about the first issue of my magazine;
I'm excited about the seventh anniversary issue.

In an old easy-chair in the living room,
the sun's over my shoulder,
the same sun.

May 9, 1983

More Serious Than Chewing Your Cuticles
But Not As Bad As Cannibalism

Consuming your exuberant feelings
by way of Sara Lee chocolate cream cake
rather than your heat-seeking eros missile system,
    or a game of softball, some beers afterwards
at Dave's Foxhead, where the late afternoon sun pours
as golden as Miller's High Life
through the tall early 20th century windows.

You could even have listened to the music you love
or have played your saxophone.

    Advertising agencies know about this quirk
of human nature and its manifestations
in Consumerism—and at its extreme, Gluttony,
Greed, Addiction, Personal Betrayal, and War,
and that sometimes
a glass of cold milk goes great with it.

July 1983

Ozark DC-9 Saint Louis To New York City

Unfasten the seat belt;
square your feet upon

six miles of space.

The air vent system ebbs-and-flows
like an old fan in a warehouse you worked in
when jet planes were the new thing.
—Or is it the engine that ebbs-and-flows
and is it supposed to?
    Should you report this to the pilot?
(The flight attendant might not take you seriously
after a million miles of tending to thousands of fears.)
You're the one who noticed vibrations in the old Buick
given to you and your first wife by her parents,
and pulled in to a service station on the interstate
to learn that the drive shaft was an inch
from falling out, and could have catapulted us.

    Tell the pilot?
—or write a poem
to be found, possibly, in smoldering rubble?

Outside your window: the wing,
a thirty-foot length of simple, perfect construction
the color of galvanized zinc nuts, bolts, corner braces,
mending plates, screws, spring washers and what-have-you
stored loose in drawers—not "bubble-packed"
—binding artifacts of our civilization,
objects you handled piece by piece when packing orders

and taking inventory in your father's one-man
wholesale hardware store.
   Your window reflects upon that wing, a vision
of "fish pastry" and escarole lettuce on an orange tray.
This kind of surrealism, you don't need.
You're still taken by simply *existing;* you remain a primitive
in matters of life and death, even with the existence of
a fifty-year-old flight attendant, which civilizes most people.
You prefer the living room sofa, feet upon the carpet.

   Take-off was like an intravenous blast of amphetamine
(called *speed* on the street).
And, descending to LaGuardia was indeed "coming down"
(another street term—this for the wearing-off
of drug effects, also called "crashing")
—the reduced engine revolutions and attending lower
pitch of engine sounds—perceived by an infrequent flyer
as mechanical failure—while your stomach descended
into the lower intestine).
The aircraft seemed to have stalled over a New Jersey
Con Edison landscape, hanging there
like a skyscraper elevator stuck between floors.

   You've taken all the chances you'll probably ever want to take
—*for love* in riding a motorcycle many times to Riverside, Iowa
down Highway 218, that narrow two-laner
with windy shudders of approaching semi-trailers;
—*for excitement,* as a child climbing through the
classroom window at night for cookies and cookie money;
—*as a teenager* jumping out of airplanes in the 82nd Airborne;
—*for life,* in shooting-up speed and junk in the 'sixties,
then settling into writing poetry and being a small-press publisher.

continued

Now, in the 48th year of your life—twice the age
of the average poetry-reading attendee and of your ex-wife,
and the entire life expectancy of most ancient Romans
—you should put your life on the line *for convenience*?

HERE RESTS MORTY SKLAR
WHO SAVED THIRTY-SIX HOURS ROUND-TRIP

November 1983

The Holder Of The Key

I recall the Greenwich Village of my youth
where pleasure was my joy,
and speed, weed, then heroin were the key
for my friends and me.

Years later, in Phoenix House
ex-junkies/brothers taught me
to postpone present pleasure for future pleasure;
that we were there to restore choice to our lives.
They said: Do the right thing and everything will follow.
I thought that meant I'd be happy
but I don't remember happiness being talked about.
I thought it meant I'd be free
but did anyone say what freedom was?

What I felt before I stuck that needle in my vein
—doing what's right doesn't make me feel good.

But feeling hadn't made it so
—thinking did
and thinking also made me free.
I keep my thinking someplace safe;
I am the holder of the key.

February 1984

Public Buildings

In the winter it is cold
and we go inside to warm-up.
In the summer it is cold
so we go outside to warm-up.

June 1984

Things I Thought Were Bad For Us

Competition
Hot-dogs

We want the Quad City Cubs to win
but are caught off guard
and cheer for any snappy hit
and expertly fielded ball.

When we leave the ball park
John's organic trail mix
is still unopened in his backpack.

July 1984

How A Poem Comes

Does a fish come
or do you go after a fish?
(Is dropping a line in the river
and curling your toes beneath the sun,
fishing?)

Sometimes a poem comes
and you're not there.
Did you ever think that Jesus
could be sitting next to you
at the counter in Hamburg Inn?

A poem comes like a fish,
like a savior.

June 1985

On Being A Grown-up

A man likes having become a grown up
after being an adolescent, sort of, for forty years.
But then he doesn't like it as much
when so often he must be even more grown up.
He used to think "grown up" was a place of arrival
where one enjoys the rewards (such as acceptance
of oneself and others), and takes stock of
the responsibilities (like maintaining grown-upness
in the face of adolescence).

But grown-upness, like love, is not only a state
but a job, sort of, and as such, paying attention to details
is important, whether in lathing a machine part to
within .0017 mm tolerance, or getting the dirt
out of a corner.
Well, that's okay (as it should be for a grown-up)
but then, sometimes, the man wants to call his mother,
to confide in her as a child or as a friend, but his mother
is now eighty-six and no longer a grown-up.

The man has been feeling blue, even having friends,
and dissatisfied even with his work going tolerably well.
So he is reminded to call his mother
who too, has been blue.

May 1986

Overture To Death

Each part of us is capable of listening,
and we should watch for the part that is.

Computers are nice,
the functioning of a porpoise's brain is nice,
the composition of the elements of other planets is nice,
but what is nicer than us?
What, of what we see or hear
is *not* a part of us?
And what of that we cannot see or hear?
Parts of us are watchful like radar with nothing in its range,
yet sense not *nothing*, but silence, perhaps,
like ocean waves seen from afar.

What of light, which can't be seen?
and space?

The overture to Death may be silent and invisible.
    Something's there, Mommy, in the dark.
       Hush, I'll leave a little light.
    Something is still there, Mommy.
       Hush, everything is all right.

And what of Mommy, who one day we'll no longer see?
And fear, which one day could disappear?

Who, who does not embrace life,
can embrace death?
    Did you leave your parents' house not knowing
what you'd find? Did you leave the city of your birth
not knowing what you'd find?
Did you ever leave a job not knowing what you'd find?

What have these deaths been but overtures to life?
When you weren't embraced, did you embrace?

Death could be a great furry ape
the only thing drifting toward you
as you hurtle through space
—whom you forever
then embrace.

September 1986

The Sound Of A Universe Beating

The heart performs, each second
what the universe hasn't accomplished
in two billion years.
      Chuck says there's a frequency whose sine wave
spans the continental U.S.A.

      I lost my gloves
somewhere in the universe two days ago,
probably at the movie theater. But I don't mind
part of me remaining at "The Iceman Cometh"
—I liked everything connected to it,
even my old shoes and gray beard. People
is all I don't like—a lot of people a lot of the time.

      What would it be like on earth
alone? I think I could handle it
—like having my own apartment the first time at twenty,
so free so alone with everything,
heart beating in a time that passes so quickly
that slowing it down takes kilocycles of sine waves
vibrating at my side
in a song

1987

To Station

The sky lightens
in the eastbound Zephyr club car window.
Because people don't want passenger trains, with their
associated traffic and traffickers, running through
their downtowns, we passengers are afforded
an Edward Hopper canvas stretched eleven hundred miles
from Mount Pleasant, Iowa to Grand Central Station.

Variations on brick-red generate a palette of their own,
from factories in the long-waning sunset, to barn sides
in the rising sun's bath.
A lovely place, Earth, with its peaceful flag of green
and brick-red.
Green in the countryside, green in industrial streams…
pollution is but a pimple on so vast a lovely face.

An island of hooded platform appears in the darkening sky,
and rising from it

TO STATION

with no arrows, no directions, just two
tall wooden doors painted barn red
with burnished brass handles
and many unwashed window panes awash
in dusty yellows   browns   rust and gold…

continued

The station took away the green
but gave back a hundred sunsets
in small warehouse windows.

For twenty-eight hours I neither arrive nor depart
as towns pass and the signs change
but not the colors.

June 1987

At Shakespeare & Company Bookstore, Paris
I Enter The Writer's Room, Where I'll Stay

There's a half-eaten chicken on the kitchen counter,
a broken glass on the floor between desk and chair

and floor-to-ceiling, wall-to-wall books…

I'd left for Paris from Iowa City via Jackson Heights,
Thonon-les-Bains, and a countryside of rail
crowned with snow and clouds.

   Nothing need be done in Paris this 3 a.m.
but moping, and thinking of photographs
that I wish to take.
Reading glasses, a pen, some tobacco,
Converse sneakers, a timepiece, a firm bed,
four thousand miles from home in a large room
across from Notre Dame
has me thinking of wealth
and how we come to it.

May 1988

Feeling Good—What's It Good For?

I feel good.
Feeling good is a mini-vacation.
On a regular vacation, you do things;
with a mini-, you don't have to do anything.
Not doing anything feels good when most of the time
you've been doing everything.

Feeling good—what's it good for?
If it's good for nothing,
then nothing is good enough for me.

It's good to feel good with others
but it's better to feel good alone
than to not feel good at all.

When you don't feel good
it seems that no one else does either,
so it's good for helping others feel good.

How do you get to feel good?
Beats me—I do things that sometimes make me feel good
but other times don't.
Weirdly enough, my acceptance of that feels good
—or keeps me from feeling bad.

March 1989

One Home, Many Places

I feel good this morning.
Is it because I'm better-used-to not smoking?
Is it because the temperature is 62 in late June
and the sun is now at an angle where it doesn't bake
my 12 by 15 room, and trees to the west filter its rays,
offering a wealth of coins, light greens and dark
glimmering in my windows?

   or because I dreamed last night that I held someone
in silence and steadfastness,
and though she was unsure, she did not resist?

   or because now that I have little hope for greatness,
I have greater satisfaction in smallness?

   or my having seen *The Last Temptation Of Christ*
with a friend?
   or because I *have* a friend?
   or that I'm a free man, free
to write this, free
from a life-long habit,
comfortable in my skin, earthly place of my being.

June 1989

V
You *Can* Go Home Again

Memory

back in Jackson Heights, Queens

Pulse quickens during a run on the streets…

My body's memory is no longer painful,
any more than sweating and getting out-of-breath is
—which, actually, generate that heroin-like hormone
in the brain.

      Isn't the truest memory, the body's?
During 1960 electroshock therapy, I'd become more fearful
with each session, even though I'd never felt pain
when zapped unconscious.
Yet for twenty years, whenever I pictured the electrodes
about to be touched to my moistened temples,
I shuddered.

Some body memories eventually fade,
such as mine of electroshock,
and loss of the marriage bed.

      The heart, too, remembers.
The heart, where thought and feeling get physical.

Running, heartbeat three times faster than at rest,
as it can be when you're sick or afraid
or in love.
Running-inhale running-exhale running-inhale
running-exhale memories mixing with oxygen
and glucose feeding the brain
and heart
without my knowing how.

January 1990

The Story Of My Life

I knew they'd be closed
—it was ten past five.

I went there anyhow.

Sure-enough, the door was locked.
But they let me in

June 1990

First Poem For Last Love

*It is as though I'm experiencing a
feedback loop in my harmonic
configuration.* —Data in "Star Trek"

The mysteries of space: outer-, warped-, and sub-,
are Data's milieu. How do we remain so enrapt
with each episode of "Star Trek: The Next Generation"
without comprehending the science of it?
—By the way the characters relate to the science and
to each other, the latter of which is a mystery to Data.

   Most people want to be something: a writer, a firefighter,
a Starship officer. Data, a Starship officer, wants to be
some*body*. Not somebody important, or well known,
but somebody human. He, the most advanced android ever,
"experiencing a feedback loop in my harmonic configuration,"
is as fascinating to watch in his first stirrings of romantic love
as his shipmates are in grappling with a newly-encountered
galaxy, or life-form.

   Data gives a poetry reading.
His shipmates are at best polite.
When he attempts to discover his audience's impressions,
he learns that his poetry is considered interesting
and well put-together, but too cerebral.
Was that because he's an android? Not necessarily.
He'd made the mistake most of us make
when first we write poetry: He generalized too much.

   It's funny about androids, and "Replicants" such as
the one Harrison Ford's character falls in love with
in "Blade Runner," and the Rutger Hauer character there
who is the highly evolved leader of the rebel Replicants
and is doomed, as they are, to die at age twelve:

They're basically like the rest of us, living-out life's dramas,
destined to die.

Perhaps the Replicant-detection test, based upon a
replicant's having little in his past to allow him to relate
to very common human situations (because he has no past
other than what had been implanted in his brain
by his human gods), if applied to some residents of Building P
in Creedmoor State Hospital, would result in false positives.
And by the same reasoning, if the Replicant leader
(whose last act was to spare the life of the Blade Runner,
who killed the other Replicants and mortally wounded him)
was placed side-by-side with the human who shot in the back
and killed a bicyclist in Prospect Park in Brooklyn,
the average person would guess wrong as to who
was human—though perhaps not the film-reviewing team
of Siskel and Ebert. (Of that movie, Siskel said,
"It was pretty to look at for about fifteen minutes."
Ebert disagreed, saying it was pretty enough to watch
for its entire length.) If the reviewers are human, then they
were in denial, because the Blade Runner's heart-throb's
having been a Replicant prevented them from being touched
by the quite natural and sympathetic relationship
that had evolved into love—a relationship more moving
than many between two humans, whether in the movies
or in life! And it also prevented them from paying tribute to
their kind of hero—the altruistic, passionate and courageous
leader of the Replicants.

What would Data think of my relationship to Marcela?
If he could bring on-screen my romance history,
what would he make of, on the one hand my many love poems
—even for relationships that never got started,
and on the other hand not one poem for Marcela

until today? He might understand if he saw that I wrote
the first poem for my mother when I was thirty-five
—and then only after she'd coerced me. ("You wrote such
a beautiful poem for your father—why can't you write one
for me?"), to which I'd replied, "But Mom, I'm an artist
—I can't just sit down and write a poem when somebody
asks me to," to which she'd replied,
"I'm not *somebody*—I'm your mother!"

And thus was born my first occasional poem
and a deeper understanding of poetry,
which enables me to write this today.

June 1993

Acoustical Programming Of The Day

5:30 a.m. Telephone rings—I jump out of bed to get it.
It's not my phone—it's one in a commercial
on the radio station I'd fallen asleep to.

6:00 a.m. Door bell. I ignore it—it's no doubt the
newspaper-delivery guy, whom my brother has
again failed to pay. I sympathize, but it's him or me.

6:30 a.m. Fierce high-pitched relentless bark-yapping
for a minute.

7:00 a.m. Alarm goes off—I rise quickly upon my arm,
look at the clock, then realize it's a tea kettle
in the apartment across from ours.

10:30 a.m. The day officially begins
with my brother's unveiling of his cockatiels and parakeet,
the first of which begin tentatively to whine, then build
to earnest hoots,
and the second of which sings its heart out
in the best tradition of a Disney forest-movie.
    I think: It's funny—in Iowa, machines drove me crazy
in early-morning lawn mowing frenzies,
and in New York City, birds.

Noon. The new tenant downstairs is shouting in intense anger
in the style of a basso-profundo radio announcer
at someone whose voice I never hear.

    The roof, two floors above, isn't being repaired today,
    and replacement of all the windows in the building
    has not yet begun today

and the pneumatic-hammer removal
of the concrete walkways is completed,
as is the breaking-down of walls to replace the lead pipes
that had been installed thirty-nine years ago
to conserve copper for the Korean War.

1:00 p.m. It's the daily scream-at-the-top-of-your-voice choir
in the playground on our side of the building.

Jackson Heights's tallest building, near completion two
blocks away, now only emits sounds that I can only imagine:
smoosh/mush of the bricklayer's trowel,
swish of the painter's brush.

2:00 p.m. The tune I hear every day, both now
and in the early evening and sometimes late at night
—a tune that is completely played-out in ten seconds
but is repeated again and again—Mr. Softee's
as it comes down our street, continues up and down
adjacent streets, its musical accompaniment wafting up
to our eighth-floor three-exposure windows.

1-800 blah blah blah, blah blah blah blah
—that's 1-800 blah blah blah, blah blah blah blah.
Call now. Again—dial 1-800 yap yap yap yap.
    I'm a radio-listener, you see: talk radio, news, jazz,
and so on, and maybe I get away with not buying
what they're selling, but I pay, believe me, with 800 numbers
chirp chirp chirping all the time like cockatiels!

6:00 p.m. It's Marcela calling to say she's leaving work.
She also called at 8:25 a.m. to wish me a good day
before leaving for work.
How sweet, how nice, my Marcelita.

11:00 p.m. A car alarm whoops and yelps,
guardian of the earth-polluters when they are violated by thieves
—or more often when just sat upon by teenagers
or bumped into by men with opened cans in small brown bags.

    I go to sleep with someone's voice, not Marcela's,
by my side—a radio voice. How different here
from Marcela's apartment with its sounds of sons on the phone,
dog barking alternately in impossible-to-contain frenzy
of affection and protective devotion, and Marcela's mother
calling in Spanish from her bedroom around midnight
—"What's that man's voice?" while Marcela and I watch tv.
    Some people drink warm milk, some take pills, some
read, to fall asleep. I hug my pillow next to the radio.
In my past is Captain Midnight, Inner Sanctum, Gangbusters,
The Lone Ranger…
    The phone rings.
    (Oh, yes, Marcela also calls me at her bedtime.
    It must be 11:30 now.)

July 1993

Culture

It's a cultural thing
to say *give me* a lo mein, *give me* a soda

It's a cultural thing
to swing around the corner in your livery cab,
disregarding pedestrians

    to hawk-up a wad of phlegm
in close proximity to someone
then spit it on the sidewalk, not in the gutter

    to piss next to a dumpster on my street,
in daylight, then pass the culture on to your
three-year-old by having him piss there too.

It's a cultural thing to stand on the station platform
in front of a subway-car door
then push into the wall of people trying to exit,

    to cross someone's path without as much
as looking at him.

It's a cultural thing, after taking the cabby's money,
to shoot him in the head to eliminate the witness,

    to toss a bucket of plaster off the roof
of an apartment building onto a police officer
while he's writing tickets on double- parked cars.

It's a cultural thing, our mayor's having the city pay
for the funeral of the "victim" of a policeman's bullet
—before a proper investigation revealed the "victim"

as having been an established drug dealer
in possession of a gun,

　　A cultural thing to pitch a molotov cocktail onto
a fire engine rushing into your street, brought there
with a false alarm,

　　to bash-in a man's head because he was where it was
the cultural thing for a jury to acquit policemen
doing their thing by kicking-in the ribs of a felled man
who had been doing his thing of getting stoned out of his mind
and acting-out.

It's cultural, your calling me a racist
because I didn't like your poem about culture
enough to publish it in my magazine
—or because I, a registered democrat who had voted to elect
a black mayor, this time voted in our mayoral election
for the white republican former federal prosecutor.

November 1993

My Mother Said She Was Held Back

a kaddish

My mother stopped eating.
Eating was the last sign of her tenacity,
the last expression of her passionate being
except for rare outbursts of "I love you"
or grabbing your hand or anyone's
and kissing it.

I say that first she died, then she quit eating.
What she was chewing in her last years
didn't provide the nourishment she craved.
It's amazing that she went on for so long.
Perhaps what would have killed her, had she
lived longer, also kept from her an insight
that would have caused her to despair.
Or maybe a relentless, incommunicable despair
that inhabited her being, was refracted
through the prism of her dauntless soul
into ecstasy
     or peace.

I had witnessed, fifty-four years earlier
in the Catskill Mountains, my mother leaning
over the side of a hospital bed
and into a pan that my father held,
throw-up 65% of her blood.
   I'd slowly approached her as she was wheeled
from her room, an angelic look upon her face,
a wan smile. She said to me
"Don't worry, Mickey, I'll be all right."

Our mother's food-tray card read

DOUBLE PORTIONS

and until she'd stopped eating, she scarfed every morsel
no matter what, and when the last spoonful was gone,
licked the spoon, the cups, the bowls.
If you'd put your hand on her arm then and asked,
"How's it going, Mom?"
she'd brush it aside.

"You're going to eat me out of house and home"
I would tell her, as she once told my brother and me.
She also used to say, "All I have to do is *look* at food
and I gain weight!" And for more than ten years
she'd been eating everything in sight—even off
someone else's tray when a new orderly sat her
too close to one. But her five-feet-one-inches
found its equilibrium at ninety-eight pounds.

I wonder if the plaque and snarls in her
ninety-five-year-old brain prevented her
from appreciating that irony.
I wouldn't bet on it
—I don't give up on anyone, especially she who
hadn't given up on me, even when I'd
given up on myself.

People will surprise you
—like when I'd said to my mother a year ago
when she was dressed in calf-high white socks
and a girlish dress: "Mom, you look like a schoolgirl
today," and she glanced at me, then turned her gaze
to the table top in front of her,
and shouted "Yeah!
—I was held back!"

December 1994

Blade Runner

Blade Runner, you live in a future that has the intimacy
of a rented room
where a teenager imagined he'd write a novel
—though one unlike a story such as yours.

The sirens of airborne police cars in your world
sing to me like the fog horns off Hart Island
where I kicked heroin in 1967.

Before Hart Island, my Marcela's car hung
over a precipice in the Andes mountains,
and I slumped unconscious on a toilet seat
in Horn & Hardart's, West 55th Street,
a #26 needle hanging from a vein in my arm.

　　Fires and sirens rise from our cities,
　　spirits at the dawn of life.

The Replicants' leader gave to you a lesson in love,
for he so much loved his own short life
that was programmed to last twelve years
and was shortened by your blow,
that he allowed you to live.

　　I, like him
"have seen things you wouldn't believe"
—a thousand suns setting at once
in the windows of a skyscraper,
and the pool of life floating
in the eyes of my Beloved.

July 1995

NOTICE

On August 17th, 1996 at approximately 9 p.m.
Orfelina Quintanilla de Barriga was taken
from the arms of her daughter Marcela
and secured in a holding pattern
in that part of God's universe encompassed by her bed
and 1,500 cubic feet of space...

>   *Moments earlier, twenty minutes into our watching*
>   *"Jules and Jim," Marcela had gone to her mother's room*
>   *and returned shortly.*
>   *"Morty, I think my mother is dead."*

...and secured by our Lady of the animals, who had strayed
from her established watchdog place for the first time
and never entered Orfelina's room all evening...

...by the painting above her bed, of her husband
Juan Jose—his appearance to me initially of a stern
revolutionary, changed into one of a man who
for thirty years had steadfastly guarded a place
beside himself for his wife...

...by the arrival of Patricio and Marcos, her grandchildren
who had also become her children while Marcela
and their father struggled in the New World...

...by the rosary Marcela laid on Orfie's breast,
and by a newly lighted Saint Anthony candle
and ninety-five-year-old dolls in the alcove near her bed,
side-by-side with Catholic icons...

...by the arrival of police and a paramedic,

and their detailed documentation…

…by our calls to the funeral home, and to relatives and
friends in Jackson Heights, Manhattan, New Jersey,
Chicago, California, Peru.

    We are approached by God's emissary
    and a cross eight feet tall
as we carry Orfelina up the aisle at Saint Bartholomew's
in the Elmhurst childhood neighborhood
of her grandchildren, the cross a moment before only a
symbol to me, a Jew, but now a meeting place.
    Orfelina is rising, my rising heart informs me
as it enters a holding pattern at the priest's opening prayers
and a woman's voicing of "Ava Maria"
—all in Spanish, the words of which I don't understand,
the eyes and voice of the priest which I do.

    Marcela's eyes are drowning;
    her thigh against mine is hot;
    in my hand is a throbbing wounded bird,
    her hand.

The priest disperses incense above and around Orfelina,
anoints her with Holy Water,
and she leaves us
with one another.

August 1996

Flor Andina

She played basketball,
loves country music and opera,
used to belly-dance,
and sees in cranky people like myself
and her dog-pound mutt, Lady,
the fragile child and pup.

Mi flor Andina, my flower of the Andes,
as a young woman danced to Glenn Miller
in her birthplace in Peru, while I listened
to the same on the radio
in Elmhurst, New York City.

She came to the U.S. in the same year
I emigrated from the Land of Nod,
both of us embarking on new lives,
then meeting in the building
where we both live.

Citizens then, for twenty-five years,
our immigrant hearts embraced.

October 1997

My Selmer Mark VI Alto Saxophone

I don't recall if I'd *played* "All The Things You Are"
or just sang the beginning and hummed
and scatted the rest.

I can't say that Rick, Doug, Audrey, Dr. Dick, Carlos,
Dan, Chuck, Jim and I and whoever else might show up
had played *songs* when we jammed at the bungalow
that Rick bought for $5,000 in Iowa City
on Bowery Street between Gilbert and Linn

—or in the downtown Mini Park before the new
Godfather's Pizza boosted the economy but took from us
the park's ambience by removing the bushes
we'd played among

—or at Carlos's pad, so small for our congas and bongos,
the saxophone, guitars—both electrified and acoustic,
the Goodwill toy piano and kazoo, and we singing,
chanting, shouting stomping,
fueled by weed, espressos, friendship, youth, and freedom.

No, not whole songs did we play, even when Carlos and
Jim—real musicians—kicked us off with one.
      But it *was* music, once we got-up a head of steam,
or, call it "good enough for jazz," but whatever,
"They Can't Take That Away From Me".

      I confess—I never played a song in its entirety.
I played scales in the back of my father's store after hours,
and in my first apartment at 81st and Columbus
in Manhattan; then I played the pawn shop tune
to cop heroin, and the parents jingle when I gave to mine
the pawn tickets for their wedding silverware.

I always held on to my saxophone tickets,
and one day I was again practicing scales:
In my Prospect Park West Brooklyn basement apartment
after graduating from the Phoenix House drug program,
and then in a $40 a month room on West 20th
before leaving New York—where my next-door Basque
neighbor tried to push my door in when he'd
lost his job and came home drunk in the afternoon
wanting to sleep it off.

I practiced in Iowa City in some of the twelve
places I'd lived, the last of which was the home
of Jack's and Shirley's, who'd invited me to stay until
I could load all my possessions on a Ryder rental truck
and move back to New York.
I took music lessons from Jim Mulac until the day
Jack said, "Morty, are you *ever* going to New York?"

Now, for Marcela I sometimes play my sax
to salsa or jazz that's on the radio or a record,
and I play the flute she brought me from Perú,
and the pan flute she bought me in Russia.
I listen to a lot of radio programs—from
alternative medicine to politics, personal and financial
counseling, religion…
One day when all the words begin to sound like noise,
I hit the Newark jazz station and take out my sax
to join in.

"My musician,"
Marcela says.

December 1997

Nap

"I'm going to take a nap," Marcela says.

When I return from the Empire with fried fish
and tostones, she comes out of the bedroom.
"I thought you were tired," I say.
   "No," she says–"why?"
"Because you said you were going to take a nap."
   "A nap, yes, but I'm not tired."
"What is a nap?" I ask.
   "When you lie down and read a book, or watch tv
or something," she replies.
"You don't know what a nap is! I almost shout.
   She and I had taken a few naps together,
and at times I'd gone to my room, saying I was going
to take a nap, and asked her to wake me if I slept more
than half an hour.

I was reminded of having discovered
when we were together three years,
that she thought authors *paid* me to publish them.
   "How could you think that?" I'd asked.
But even as I uttered those words I thought, yeah,
why would somebody put in so much time
to publish other people's work if there wasn't enough
money in it to just pay the rent?

   I went to my desk and opened the dictionary
   for the definition of "nap."

May 1998

The Gap

The gap between The Gap's image
and my pants made by The Gap
—or for The Gap in Indonesia:
    First, the color—not really chinos or
army-issue khaki, and yet not really beige
or grey. That takes me back forty years
to Klein's bargain basement at Union Square,
where the prices were great (unlike The Gap's)
and the styles okay—but all the colors were just
a bit off—enough so that I'd end-up
not buying the $29.95 woolen suit or $5.95 pants
that had lured me there.

These Gap pants were a gift,
which is why I've kept them
—and as a pair of utility pants, I thought they'd be fine
even having to turn-up the thirty-inch cuffs (my size)
to keep my heel off them.
And the feel of them is so unlike 100% cotton
that I had to look at the label to confirm they were.

    Worst of all are the short pockets
—a very unluxurious feeling when you can't plunge
your hands into your pants pockets.
But they were okay around the apartment
—until my pen disappeared, only to turn-up months later
between the living room couch cushions.

    I'm not a person to get rid of things easily,
whether an old bedspread (good drop cloth for painting)
or the kosher turkey's metal button with its
Hebrew lettering, which I'd clipped to my shirt sleeve
when I served Thanksgiving dinner to guests.   *more*

What could I have done the day I was out the door
in a rush for an appointment and realized
as I reached for my wallet and felt the top of my pen
protruding fromthe pants pocket,
that I should have changed my pants?
    In the subway I felt the tops of my pants pockets
as I sat down, for any protrusions (I'd already moved
the pen to my shirt pocket).
    At my appointment I checked again

    and again on the way home on the 23rd Street
cross-town bus.
    As the bus approached Park Avenue, I moved toward
the rear exit to transfer to the #6 train.
I had to squeeze through a couple of passengers,
one of whom was obstinate in not turning his angled body
to accommodate me. With my third and most emphatic
excuse me, I glared at him and said to the woman on my
other side, "What's wrong with him?"

I stepped to the street and reached for my wallet
for the Metrocard.
The familiar bulge, the bulge of a lifetime, one that
had been there since I'd heeded a warning as a young man
to not keep my wallet in a back pocket,
WAS GONE—as though I'd had a pocketectomy.
I couldn't have felt worse short of sustaining bodily damage
or losing my Nikon F camera
—until I reached into my other pants pocket
to discover that *my credit-card–and-photo billfold* was gone!

    On the #7 train to Queens, which I'd boarded
    with the change at the bottom of my pants pocket,

there was a gap in my gut.
I became one of those crazy New Yorkers,
saying repeatedly to the air in front of me:
"I was robbed! Someone picked my pockets!
I'll be sixty-five in a month and finally I'm the one
whose pockets were picked."

   By the time we reached the 61st Street Woodside
station, another part of me
was grateful
that all that had been taken from my life
were my wallet and billfold.

November 2000

Rold Gold Snack Mix—Guaranteed Fresh

(offered to us by an airline)

Bleached and unbleached flour
partially hydrogenized soybean oil
partially hydrogenized canola oil
sugar, corn syrup, partially hydrogenized corn oil
sodium bicarbonate, ammonium bicarbonate
monocalcium phosphate, disodium phosphate
disodium inosinate, disodium guanylate, maltodextrin,
partially hydrogenized cottonseed oil, dextrose
artificial colors (yellow 6, yellow 5, caramel color)
distilled soy monoglycerides, autolyzed yeast
hydrolyzed soy protein, hydrolyzed wheat gluten
protease, sodium sulfite

June 2001

Waiting

From my chair in Starbucks
I can see where 8th Street becomes Saint Mark's Place,
and 3rd Avenue becomes Bowery.

I came here after having purchased quinoa pasta
and freshly-ground peanut butter at Prana's grocery,
1st Avenue and 7th Street, then a falafel sandwich on pita
at a mid-eastern joint on Saint Mark's,
and a Rolling Rock beer next door to it at Dojo's.
  I still have a couple of hours to kill.

  I must say—viewed from my easy-chair,
the floor-to-ceiling windows overlooking both streets
are a splendid spot to wait for my black-&-white
Peru-trip photographs being finished across town
at Spectra, where I had arrived three hours too early
  —God's way of getting me to relax,
or as my woman champions, "waste time."

  Where the yellow and red McDonald's arch is
across the street, Thelonius Monk once wailed
at the Five Spot in the early 1960s.
You may be able to extrapolate from that, other changes
here in east Greenwich Village thirty-eight years later.

As for myself, I still write poems and I still look at girls
  —their breasts, their hips, hair, walks, expressions, clothes,
their boyfriends—or girlfriends…
but I don't feel anymore that urgency to have them,
though that would be nice.

continued

I'm married to an ex-girl—which lends new meaning
to our having called our girlfriends, back then,
our "old ladies."

I lean back to pay attention to the flavor of my coffee,
no longer waiting.

July 2001

Nine One One

a few miles from ground-zero

On Sunday we watched "Triumph Of The Spirit,"
    a story of the Holocaust.
On Monday we saw "Traffic," the war on drugs.
On Tuesday we witnessed the World Trade Center
    twin towers collapse.

    A man and woman held hands,
    leapt from the upper floors.

    Woman to a reporter: "I want to dig him out
    with my hands—what if he's dying and I
    can't hold him in my arms?"

On waking this morning I felt that some part
of my body was missing.
New York City, the United States of America,
yesterday stepped on a land mine and lost a limb.

    Hijacker to passenger on American Airlines
    flight 11: "Call your wife and tell her
    you're going to die."

Repetition of video footage: planes crashing
    into both towers, fire
and the genie-like cloud of smoke hovering
about its wounds, then crashing to the streets
with the upper floors…

repetition of verbal reportage
and anecdotal accounts, repetition as with
the O.J. Simpson murder trial

and in automobile ads, cereal ads, deodorant ads,
and in news that is not news…
repetition that has infuriated me more and more
the older I get

…now becomes a rosary of reiteration
like my father's in synagogue on Yom Kippur,
his words repeated, "Boruch atoh Adonoy, Elohaynu
Melech ho-olom…Blessed art Thou O Lord our God…,"
his repeated bows from the waist, his fist upon his chest…

repetition we don't seem to tire of
—not only because the event is too momentous
to grasp all at once,
but because we're here to tell about it.

September 11, 2001

Brad Mehldau At Carnegie Hall

I tell Marcela that my Charlie Parker T-shirt
is in the laundry basket, or else I'd wear it.
She—who never tells me what I should wear,
rarely even hints at it—says, "You ought to wear
a shirt and tie to Carnegie Hall."
    "But it's a jazz concert," I say.
"It doesn't matter," she says, "—it's Carnegie Hall."
I tell her I'm usually over-dressed at prestigious halls,
that even guys my age don't wear jackets or ties.
    She says nothing.

I consider my Ellis Island T-shirt with its hundred flags,
but put on a starched shirt, tie and jacket
and feel okay about it.

    At Carnegie Hall, Brad and his trio are introduced,
    and come onto the stage
    all wearing T-shirts.

July 2002

Why America
(or as my Peruvian wife corrected me,
The United States Of North America) Is Great

because you can have grown up where practically everyone
    spoke English—even your father who came from Russia,
    then end-up at sixty-nine back there in Jackson Heights,
    Queens, *noticing* when someone is speaking English...
because you are free
    to spit your gum onto the sidewalk
    drop trash on the escalator or toss it into the train tracks,
    deposit your empty or partially filled soda bottle or cup
        on the subway platform or under a subway car seat,
    blow your nose and hawk-up phlegm in the gym shower...

speak Spanish, Urdu, Korean, Russian, Hindi, Adinfinitum
    on the street, in the bus, stores, the doctor's waiting room
    and even to me as you hand out flyers on the street corner;
    and listen to it on the radio in your stores, where I shop...

speak *loudly* to that plastic thing you hold to your ear
    in all the aforementioned places.

    I told my wife I'm not just being cranky
    —that my reaction is visceral like Cosmo Kramer's
    in the "Seinfeld" episode where he convulses
    whenever he hears the voice of tv host Mary Hart.
        My wife, who's known me for thirteen years,
    asks that I consider taking medication.

I'd rather become a hermit
or be pissed-off for so long that I have to do something,
like write.

America is great because I can come home to privacy
and intimacy, and not hear a foreign language spoken
—except when my wife is on the phone, my sweet wife.
America is great because here is where I found her.

August 2005

Text is typeset in Minion, *Minion italic*,
Minion semibold, **Minion bold**,
MINION EXPERT, and **MINION EXPERT SEMIBOLD**;

Poem and section titles, in ITC Franklin Gothic Book
and *ITC Franklin Gothic Book italic;*
Book title, in LITHOS REGULAR;
ornaments, in Adobe Woodtype Ornaments 1 & 2;
The Spirit That Moves Us Press name, in *Mistral*.

Typeset in Microsoft Word 2001 for Macintosh,
and imported into QuarkXPress 4.11 for Macintosh
in an eMac running Classic in Mac OS 10.4.11,
and prepared for the printer with
Adobe Acrobat Distiller 3.0.2.

Executed at the World Headquarters of
The Spirit That Moves Us Press
in Jackson Heights, Queens,
New York City